FOR NEW RICE MILLERS; TO AVOID MISTAKES AND SAVE MONEY $

HOW TO PLAN A MONEY PRINTING RICE MILL

"Kill the possibilities of all mistakes, before they kill your dream project"

FOR NEW RICE MILLERS; TO AVOID MISTAKES AND SAVE MONEY $

"Kill the possibilities of all mistakes, before they kill your dream project"

AMIT AGGARWAL

PENDOWN PRESS
Powered by **Gullybaba Publishing House Pvt. Ltd.,**
An ISO 9001 & ISO 14001 Certified Co.,
Regd. Office: 2525/193, 1st Floor, Onkar Nagar-A, Tri Nagar,
Delhi-110035
Ph.: 09350849407, 09312235086
E-mail: info@pendownpress.com
Branch Office: 1A/2A, 20, Hari Sadan, Ansari Road,
Daryaganj, New Delhi–110002
Ph.: 011-45794768
Website: PendownPress.com

First Edition: 2022
Price: ₹999/-
ISBN: 978-93-5554-191-8

Layout and Cover Designed by Pendown Graphics Team
Printed and Bound in India by Thomson Press India Ltd.

This Book is
Dedicated to
Almighty God
My Gurus
My Parents
My Family

Contents

Introduction

When I was about to pass out of school, I saw a photograph in the newspaper that shocked me. Kevin Carter's Pulitzer Prize-winning photograph of a starving child and a vulture in the background. I could not believe that people still died of starvation.

I thought that I would definitely do something about it one day.

When I planned to start my manufacturing unit, I realized that I had made many mistakes, leading to a waste of time, money, and energy.

We started Food Grain manufacturing machines in 2008 as I thought by doing so I would be able to bridge the gap between available options and expectations in this segment.

I found that aspiring Rice Millers were making the similar mistake that I made when I had started my manufacturing unit. (They seek guidance from mill operators, fabricators and other people who, because of their personal interest and unbaked knowledge, cause them enormous losses).

This prompted me to do the required research and write a book to make people aware of the methodology involved in the project planning and management of Rice Mills, which otherwise leads to loss of time, money, energy and sometimes even the Project's failure.

I promise that this book will empower the new Rice Miller with knowledge and insight that can save them at least Rs.20 Lakhs in future losses.

Rice is the most widely consumed staple food. I am on a mission to help Rice Millers serving the entire society by processing Rice for over half of the world's population.

By doing this, I believe I will be able to contribute in some way to my bigger goal of creating a starvation free world.

Chapter 1

Core Planning

When I started my manufacturing unit, I found that I had missed adding many machines that are a must to run the plant profitably, and no one, including my consultant, had guided me to do that. Later on, I added those machines, exceeding my budget and also had to make alterations in the layout to accommodate the additional ones.

In the same way, I found that machinery sellers often don't tell the new Rice Miller about the total machine requirement (especially those out of their scope) because they fear that it will make them lose the order. Ultimately, the Rice Miller has to buy these machines later, creating similar inconveniences and losses as I went through.

In this chapter, I will share complete knowledge of all the items required for the core planning of the Rice Mill project. I will also show you how to create Purchase and Job work agreements to avoid future disputes between the buyer and seller.

This chapter will cover the following topics:

1. A comprehensive list of all the items required to complete the Project.
2. The procedure of buying & the format of the Purchase Order with all the terms and conditions.
3. Drafting and executing the Installation Agreement.

1. **List of Items needed to kick-start the Project:**

    i. **Boiler:** The objective of the Boiler is to generate the steam required for the Parboiling and Drying Process.

    Pressure required - 10.54Kg/cm2

    Capacity in Tons - For Parboiled Rice, it is equal to the Paddy Milling capacity per hour. For Steamed Rice, it is approximately 50% of the Paddy Milling capacity per hour.

    (It is a thumb rule calculation - Always take suggestions from the Boiler company before buying because Boilers of different companies operate at different efficiencies)

    ii. **Boiler Accessories:** Along with the Boiler, the following accessories are generally provided by the Boiler company:

   a. ID Fan.
   b. FD Fan.
   c. Feed Pump.
   d. Fuel Feeder.

iii. **Additional Accessories required** along with the Boiler are:

   a. Water Treatment Plant.
   b. Chimney, Flue Duct, Dust collector, Heat Recovery Unit.
   c. Interconnecting Ducting of Preheater.
   d. Fuel Handling System up to the Screw Feeder of the Boiler.
   e. Feed water tank and Feedwater Piping up to the terminal point.
   f. Steam Blowdown and Drain Piping from the Terminal Valves on the Boiler.
   g. Insulation of the Boiler and the Steam Pipeline.
   h. Refractory items for the Boiler.
   i. Structural Material-Platform, Ladder and Support.
   j. Electrical work & Cables up to the terminating point.
   k. Steam Flow Meter.

iv. **Parboiling/Steaming:** The objective of Parboiling & Steaming is to gelatinize the Rice, which leads to better nutritional value and less brokenness during Milling.

For Parboiling, it is generally 12 x (Milling Capacity per hour).

But if our objective is only Steaming, it is 3 x Milling Capacity.

(It is a thumb rule calculation - Always take suggestions from the suppliers before buying because different companies operate at different efficiencies)

v. **Dryer:** After Parboiling & Steaming, the moisture % age in the Paddy goes up to 35%, which is not suitable for Milling. A Dryer is needed to reduce the moisture and bring it to 12-13%.

   For Parboiled Rice, it is generally 12 x Milling Capacity per hour, but if it is only of Steam Rice, it is 8 x Milling Capacity.

   (It is a thumb rule calculation - Always take suggestions from suppliers before buying because different companies operate at different efficiencies)

vi. **Parboiling & Dryer Accessories:**

   a. Steam pipeline with insulation.
   b. The header for steam distribution.

      (Total length/Quantity will vary according to the project layout and capacity of the plant)

vii. **Precleaning:** A Precleaner machine is required to dress the Paddy before Parboiling & Drying and remove coarse impurities like crop residues, stones, mud balls, gunny bag threads and fine impurities like dust and immature grains.

It is suggested to install a Cleaner of capacity 16-20 Tons/hr. (Higher capacity is better as it reduces the time required to fill the parboiling tank and thus reduce the overall time needed for the Parboiling & Drying process)

viii. **Elevators & Conveyors:** One Elevator is required to take the Paddy from the houdi pit and feed it to the Precleaner.

Conveyors/Elevators are required to collect Paddy from the Precleaner and feed it to Parboiling and then move it to the Dryer.

Then the Paddy is fed to the Conditioning Silos. (Quantity required will be as per the design provided by the Parboiling and Dryer company. In most cases, the Conveyors and Elevators of the Parboiling machine & Dryer are included in the package. Ensure this before releasing the orders).

ix. **Conditioning Tanks/Silos:** The objective of the Conditioning Tank/silos is to allow the natural cooling of Paddy before Milling.

It can be constructed on-site, or readymade silos can be installed.

The capacity of each Silo should be more or equal to each Dryer, and quantities should be at least 1+ the total no. of Dryer (for smooth feeding of Paddy to Milling).

x. **Belt Conveyor:** One or two Belt Conveyors are required (as per layout) to collect the material from the conditioning silos and carry the Paddy to Milling.

xi. **Milling:** Milling involves the following sections

   a. Cleaning
   b. Milling
   c. Grading
   d. Material Handling
   e. Color Sorting
   f. Accessories

S.no.	Machine	Purpose
	Cleaning	
01	Paddy Cleaner	For size-wise cleaning of Paddy Qty-1
02	Destoner	For gravity wise cleaning of Paddy and removing stones that are of the same size as of Paddy. Qty-1 or 2 depending on the Milling Plant capacity.

	Milling	
03	Dehusker	For removing the husk layer from the Paddy surface to get Brown Rice. 1 Dehusker has a production capacity of around 3-4 tons, so accordingly, quantities are decided. Normally the Husker settings are maintained to Dehusk 90-95% Paddy in case of Parboiled Paddy and 80-85% in case of raw Paddy to avoid damage to Rice.
04	Husk Aspirator	A Dehusker machine is installed above the Husk Aspirator. The purpose of the Husk Aspirator is to blow away the husk from Brown Rice coming out of the Dehusker. Qty required, the same as the Dehusker
05	Paddy Separator	The purpose of the Paddy Separator machine is to separate residual Paddy and brown Rice coming from the Dehusking unit.
06	Oversizer	Oversizer is an optional machine that separates any oversize Rice (in terms of thickness) before whitener.
07	Whitener	2 to 4 Whiteners are used in series to buff the Brown Rice surface and remove the bran layer to get White Rice.

08	Silky Polisher	The Silky Polisher is useto polish the buffed White Rice to give it a smooth, shiny, silky surface. In general, 1 or 2 passes are given.
	Grading	
09	Rotary Shifter	Rotary Shifter is used to remove the small broken Rice before silky Polisher.
10	Undersizer	Undersizer is used to remove unmatured and dead grains (usually undersized in terms of thickness) before the Color Sorting machine. It helps reduce the load on the Sorting machines and improve the quality.
11	Length Grader	This machine is used for lengthwise grading of Rice.
	Sorting	
12	Color Sorter	Color Sorter sorts the grain's color and removes the discolored and damaged grains in rejections.
13	Compressor	Compressed air is required in Color Sorters for Operating Ejectors, although it is also required in small proportions in Husker, Silky, and Pneumatic Slide Gates.

14	UPS/CVCF	Color sorter is an electromechanical machine, and electrical fluctuations can damage the electronic circuit inside. To control the fluctuations, UPS/CVCF is used before color sorting.
15	Air Conditioner	An Air Conditioner keeps the color sorter cabin cool to safeguard electronic circuits from excessive heat.
	Material Handling	
01	Elevator	Elevators convey material vertically and feed it to the next machine in the line.
02	Screw Conveyor	A Screw Conveyor conveys the husk/ Rice mainly in a horizontal direction.
03	Chain Conveyor	Chain Conveyors are usually used in Rice mills to carry the Rice/Paddy to multiple discharge points.
04	Belt Conveyor	Belt Conveyors are used to carry the Paddy/Rice to a single discharge point. They are safest to use in terms of Rice breakage problems during conveying.

	Accessories	
01	Motors	For driving all machines
02	Blower	Centrifugal Fans are used in Rice mills. The objective of blowers is to create the necessary vacuum required for that particular machine.
03	Cyclones	Cyclones are used to collect the Bran and dust sucked by generating a vacuum through blowers.
04	Airlock	As the name suggests airlock, locks the air to flow inside the cyclone but allows the material to flow outside.
05	Bran Centrifugal	The Bran centrifugal collects the Bran from the Silky and Whitener and segregates broken Rice and Husk from the Bran.
06	S-Bend system	The S-Bend is used to segregate broken Bran or broken Husk.
07	Magnets	Magnets are used to remove iron particles, nut-bolts, etc., which may otherwise go inside the machine and damage it.

08	Pneumatic Slide Gates	Pneumatic Slide Gates are used to stop the flow of material (Paddy/ Rice) inside the machine when the electricity goes off; otherwise, it will create a Jam in the machine.
09	Chain Slide Gate	Chain Slide Gates are used to manage the flow of material by an operator manually.
10	Pipelines	Pipelines are required for the free flow of material from the discharge point of one machine/elevator to the feeding point of the next elevator/ machine through gravity.
11	Ducting	Ducting allows the flow of air/bran/ dust from the machine to the aspiration system in a controlled path, thus maintaining the required pressure and volume.
12	Spoutings	This includes T, Y, Kali, Rings, Clamps required along with pipelines for making connectivity easier.
13	Weighing Bridge	For measuring the weight of incoming Paddy and outgoing Rice and Bran.
14	Lab Equipments	Lab Cleaner, Lab Dehusker, Lab Polisher, Moisture Meter.

	Electrical Work	
1	Transformer	
2	LT Panel	
3	Power Factor Controller	
4	Cables	
5	Cable Tray & Accessories	
6	MCC Panel	
7	Earthing	
8	Electrical Fitting (Lighting, Fan etc.)	
	Consumables & Spares	
1	Rubber Roll	For Dehusker
2	Milling Roll	For Silky
3	Sieves & Blades	For the Whitener, Silky, Cleaner & Destoner
4	Motor & Gearbox	1 or 2 set for Elevators and Conveyors
5	Bearing	For the Whitener, Silky, Husker& Elevators
6	Belt & Bucket	For elevators

2. **The procedure of buying:** The procedure of buying includes the following steps:
   - **i.** Establishing the complete requirements.

     In this step, you have to analyze your:
     a. Expectations,
     b. Budget,
     c. Variety: (Long grain/Short grain) you will run.
     d. Capacity - that you want to go for.
     e. Type of Rice - Raw/Boiled/Steam.
     f. Accordingly, it would be best if you decide the complete configuration of your plant.
   - **ii.** Finalizing suppliers and handling negotiation.

     Steps:
     a. Research Technical specifications and freeze your requirements accordingly.
     b. Take feedback from suppliers and other users regarding the quality and after-sales support.
     c. Check whether the supplier provides all the required accessories (often, the supplier keeps things hidden, which puts an extra financial burden later on).
     d. **Negotiate:** Negotiation & bargaining are different things. Most of the time, we start bargaining, ignoring other aspects. Negotiation is buying the right quality and quantity at the RIGHT PRICE (not low price-please avoid this mistake). The deal should be a win-win situation for both parties. Win-lose situations create lose-lose situations at a later stage.

iii. Releasing the Purchase Order is the most important but most ignored part. Always release the detailed Purchase Order mentioning all the specifications (or you can attach the specifications provided by the supplier as mutually agreed) and mentioning all terms and conditions.

Check out the sample draft below.

<table>
<tr><th colspan="2">Sagar Nutriments Pvt. Ltd.</th><th>GSTIN: 23AAVCS7528M1ZJ</th></tr>
<tr><td colspan="3">Vill. Tamot, Tehsil - Goharganj, Obedullaganj to Goharganj Road (NH-12), Distt. Raisen-464993 (M.P.)</td></tr>
<tr><td colspan="3">PURCHASE ORDER</td></tr>
<tr><td>M/s
AGROMACH ENGINEERING PRIVATE L.T. D</td><td>Purchase Order #</td><td>430</td></tr>
<tr><td>JARU ROAD, NEAR SECTOR 59,</td><td>PO Dated</td><td>04.01.2022</td></tr>
<tr><td>BALLABGARH,</td><td>Your Quotation #</td><td>MAIL</td></tr>
<tr><td>FARIDABAD,</td><td>Quotation Dated</td><td>04.01.2022</td></tr>
<tr><td>HARYANA</td><td></td><td></td></tr>
<tr><td colspan="3">Kind Attention - MR. S.S. NEGI
Contact Number - 8800899179
Contact Email - sales@agromachengineering.com
Subject - ORDER OF GRADER AND SIZER
Department - Milling</td></tr>
</table>

Material Description	UOM	Qty	Unit Rate	Discount %	Amount (Rs.)
PE-Length Grader With input-output pipeline same as cataday with IE-3 motor Make Siemens, Gear Box-Bonifig	LOT	9.00			
Hard chrome Indent Cylinder-Sieve size#20 (8mm)-2 NOS, #11 (4.5mm)-3 NOS	NOS	5.00			
PE-Sizer (Cylinder -6, Motor Rating-2 HP, Motor Make Crompton/Siemens With IE-3, Jali Size-1.4mm)	NOS	1.00			
PE-Sizer (Addition 2 Segment in OLD M/c) Including Fabrication work	NOS	1.00			
Sizer Spring Support Rod Small	NOS	4			
Sizer Spring Support Rod Big	NOS	4			
Sizer Aluminum Triangle	NOS	2			
			Basic price (INR)		
AMOUNT IN WORDS: One Million Eighty Two Thousand Two Hundred and Twenty Five					

Terms & Conditions			
1	Freight:	Ex Shop	
2	P & F Charges:	Included. Goods should be securely packed to avoid damage & pilferage in transit	
3	Insurance:	Included	
4	Payment Terms:		10%
	Balance Payment after 30 days of material receipt		75%
	Balance Payment after 30 days of material receipt		
5	Delivery Period:	Within 7 Days	
6	Warranty:	N/A	
7	EPCG:	N/A	
8	Government Taxes:	GST 5%	
9	Delivery/Invoicing Address:	"Sagar Nutriments Pvt. Ltd." Vill.Tamot, Tehsil-Goharganj, Obedullaganj to Jabalpur Road (NH-12), Distt. Raisen-464993 (M.P.)	
10	Billing/Invoicing Address:	"Sagar Nutriments Pvt. Ltd." Vill.Tamot, Tehsil-Goharganj, Obedullaganj to Jabalpur Road (NH-12), Distt. Raisen-464993 (M.P.)	
11	Price Escalation:	The prices mentioned above are fixed & firm for all purposes and no escalation.	
12	Unloading Charges:	In SNPL Scope	
13	Inspection:	We reserve the right to inspect the material at your site before dispatch.	
14	Control Regulation:	This supply and despatch should be arranged in strict conformity with any control regulation application and after obtaining necessary permits.	
15	Jurisdiction:	All disputes subject to Bhopal jurisdiction only.	
16	Others:	Material not found as per order or agreed specifications are liable to be returned to supplier at their risk. Freight Cost, Duties and Taxes for rejected material will be debited to supplier's account.	

Kindly return a duly signed copy of this Purchase Order as a token of your acceptance and arrange timely delivery of Thanking you.		
Prepared by	Verified by	For SAGAR NUTRIMENTS PVT. LTD.
Manager (Store)	HOD	Executive Director

3. **Installation Agreement:** The following format can be used for making an agreement with the Installation contractor (If it is different from the supplier)

   Here is a draft for your reference:

   Job work Agreement between ABC and XYZ.

   This agreement is made on 21st September 2021 between:

   i. ABC having its office at XXXXXXXXX

      herein after called the First Party

      and

   ii. EFGH Director of Messrs. XYZ, incorporated under the Companies Act, 1956, having its registered office at .... India hereinafter called the Second Party.

      Whereas the First Party, the Job worker, is engaged in installing Rice Mill Plants.

      And whereas the Second Party has its own establishment and is making machinery for Rice Mills and doing Turnkey Projects.

      And whereas the Second Party, after considering the proposals put forward by the First Party, has decided to appoint the First Party as their Job Work Partner for the installation of a Rice Mill at......... with a capacity of...... Ton per Day.

Now, this agreement witnesses as:

i. The Second Party will supply the raw material like mild steel structure, sheet, plate, pipe and stainless-steel sheet/pipe, plate, flat, pipe etc., for platform fabrication & installation of machines at the customer end at XXXX.

ii. That the First Party will complete the fabrication work as per drawings & mutually agreed to conditions.

iii. The rate of Job Work would be Rs. …... Lakhs. The scope of work would include the following:

   a. Structure work
   b. Tanks fabrication and installation
   c. Elevator and Conveyor installation
   d. Machine installation
   e. Ducting
   f. Pipeline work
   g. Dust line work
   h. Trial Run

iv. That the First Party is bound to complete all the work within 150 days of reaching the customer's premises.

v. Payment terms for Erection Commissioning work would be as follows:

   a. 1st Advance before Visit........../
   b. 2nd - 15-20 days after reaching the customer's site........../

c. 3rd After 1 Month of the 2nd instalment ..../
d. 4th After 2 Months of the 2nd instalment ..../
e. 5th After 3 months of the 2nd instalment ..../
f. 6th After 4 months of the 2nd instalment ..../
g. 7th After 5 months of the 2nd instalment ..../
h. 8th After the Trial Run & Customer satisfaction ..../

vi. All travel/food expenses of the First Party and the team will be in the scope of the second Party.

In witness whereof, the parties have executed these present on the day, month and year first above written.

For ABC

For XYZ

Mr. EFGH

Resolution dated ....

In the presence of

Mr. ....

Mr. ....

Chapter 2

Time Management

When I started my unit, I failed miserably in time planning. The Laser cutting and bending machines had arrived from Japan, and our shed was not ready to keep the machines safely, which led to the late start of the Project.

The same things happen in Rice Mill projects also. Delays in the completion of the Project lead to financial losses.

Time management is the act of managing the time spent and progress made on the project tasks and activities. Excellent time management requires planning, scheduling, monitoring, and controlling all project activities.

The Seven Main Processes in Project Time Management

Plan Schedule Management: Many resources don't mention this process when discussing time management. But, before you can begin on and complete the other steps, you need to plan how you will manage your schedule.

Define Activities: Once you have your time management plan in place, you can identify and define your project activities. Major milestones should also be determined and set.

Sequence Activities: Now that you know all of the tasks that must be completed, you can start sequencing them in the proper order.

Estimate Resources: In project management, the term 'resources' often refers to people. However, you also need to identify which tools, materials, systems, Budget, and other resources you will need to complete each task.

Estimate Durations: Once you know which tasks must be completed and what you need to accomplish them, it's time to estimate how long it will take to complete each activity.

Develop the Project Schedule: This can be done by inputting your activities, their durations, the start and end dates, the sequence and their relationships.

Control the Schedule: Once your schedule is created, it needs to be monitored and controlled. Progress needs to be reviewed and updated regularly so you can compare the actual work completed against the plan. This allows you to see areas where you're falling behind schedule.

Time Management Table

Add activities, break Activities further into micro activities and change the sequence as and when required.

S. No.	Activity	Start Date	End Date	Status
01	Company Registrations			
02	Inviting Quotations			
03	Finalizing all items that need to be purchased			
04	Budget Planning			

05	Project Report Preparation			
06	Arranging Finance (Bank etc.)			
07	Land Purchase			
08	Conversion of Land to Industrial (as per local Government rules and regulations)			
09	Finalizing Main Machinery Suppliers and Releasing Purchase Orders			
10	Hiring Architect and Civil Contractor			
11	Preparation of Project Layout (take inputs from Machinery Supplier)			
12	Civil Construction			
13	Purchase of Steel, Dust, Cement etc. for construction			
14	Finalizing Fabrication Contractor			
15	Purchase of Iron & Steel for Fabrication			
16	Construction of Conditioning Silos & Tanks and Platforms for Milling			
17	Finalizing all pending accessories.			

18	Delivery of Machines and Accessories from Supplier (Releasing balance payment to them as per Agreement)			
18	Recruitment of Team (Operators for Milling, Boiler, Parboiling & Dryer, Lab In-Charge, Store In-Charge, Accountant, Manager)			
20	Installation of Machinery			
21	Completion of Electrical work			
22	Arrangement of Paddy			
23	Trial Run of Machines			
24	Corrective Actions after Trial			
25	Inauguration and starting of the Project			

Chapter 3

Rice Mill Budget Planning

A project without a budget is like a car without fuel. Funding is essential to get the Project started and set all resources in motion.

The Budget for a Project is the combined costs of all activities, tasks, and milestones that the Project must fulfill. In short: it's the total amount of money you'll need to finish the Project.

Why a Project Budget is Important

There are at least three reasons to explain the importance of having a Project Budget Plan.

First, it's an essential part of securing Project funding. The numbers will tell stakeholders (Banks, Investors and Partners) exactly how much money is needed to button up the Project and when the money is needed.

Second, a well-planned budget provides the basis for Project cost control. Having an end budget estimate helps you measure the Project's actual cost against the approved Budget and see how much cost you've burned already. It will give you an understanding of how the Project is progressing and if any changes need to be made to the plan.

Third, a Project budget directly affects the company's financial viability. When calculated feasibly and with resource constraints in mind, a project budget will increase the operating margin and improve overall success.

S. No.	Task & Milestone	Estimate	Actual
01	Land		
02	Civil Work & Construction Cost		
03	All items as per list given in chapter 1		
04	Installation Cost		
05	Man Power Cost		
06	Raw Material Cost (According to-turnaround time, usually 1-3 months of Paddy stock to be kept)		
07	Freight & Taxes		
08	Professional Expenses (Advocate, Consultant, Government Registration and other Misc expenditure)		
09	Utilities (Electricity, Fuel, Water etc.)		
10a	Poly Bags (Bardana)		
10b	Consumables		
10c	Repair & Maintenance		
10d	Advertisement & Publicity		
10e	Insurance		
10f	Misc Expenses		
11	Pre-Operating Expenses (Interest, Salary etc.)		
12	Contingency Expenses (5% of the total project cost)		
	TOTAL		

Chapter 4

ROI Calculations

People often start Rice Mill Projects because some of their friends, family or acquaintances have made good money from them. However, they mostly miss working out the actual return on their investment; they must weigh whether the Project is economically viable?

Most of the time, consultants prepare this to get funding approvals from banks and other financial partners. I recommend doing the basic calculations yourself because if a problem arises, the Banks merely risk losing their money, but for you, your money, future aspirations, emotions, everything is at stake. I have simplified all these basic calculations for you.

What is Return on Investment (ROI)?

Return on Investment (ROI) is a metric used to denote how much profit has been generated from an investment made. In the case of a business, return on investment comes in two primary forms, depending on when it's calculated: anticipated ROI and actual ROI.

Anticipated vs Actual ROI

Anticipated ROI, or expected ROI, is calculated before a Project kicks off and is often used to determine if that Project makes sense to pursue. Anticipated ROI uses estimated costs, revenues, and other assumptions to determine how much profit a project is likely to generate.

Often, this figure will be run under many different scenarios to determine the range of possible outcomes. These numbers are then used to understand risk and, ultimately, decide whether an initiative should move forward.

Actual ROI is the true return on investment generated from a project. This number is typically calculated after a project has concluded and uses final costs and revenues to determine how much profit a project produced compared to what was estimated.

Positive vs Negative ROI

When a Project yields a positive return on investment, it can be considered profitable because it yielded more revenue than it cost to pursue. On the other hand, if the Project delivers a negative return on investment, it means the Project costs more to pursue than it generated in revenue. If the Project breaks even, it means the total revenue generated by the Project matched the expenses.

Return On Investment Formula

Return on investment is typically calculated by taking the actual or estimated income from a project and subtracting the actual or estimated costs. That number is the total profit that a project has generated or is expected to generate. That number is then divided by the costs.

The formula for ROI is typically written as:

ROI = (Net Profit/Cost of Investment) X 100

ROI Calculation Table

Basis & Presumptions
The basis for calculating production capacity is on a double shift basis, working 25 days per month with 80% efficiency.
The rate of interest has been taken as 12% on average. This, however, is likely to change depending upon the location of the Project.
Labor wages have been taken based on the minimum applicable. These are likely to change depending upon the location of the Project.
Margin money usually asked by the financial institutions and banks are 15% to 25%. The entrepreneurs may check the margin money requirement from financial institutions for the Project.
Terms of loan differ from one financial institution to another, and in general, the minimum gestation period usually is 6 months-1 Year. The maximum period for repayment of the loan is 7 years, including the gestation period. The entrepreneurs from the concerned financial institutions may find the exact terms and conditions.
The cost of machinery and equipment as indicated in the scheme are approximate to those ruling at the time of preparation of the scheme. The entrepreneur may check the exact price for a specific model of the machine selected.
Non-refundable deposits, cost of preparation of project reports etc., may be considered under preoperative expenses.

The provisions made in other respects, viz; raw materials, utilities, overheads etc., are drawn based on standard variation and output. The costs indicated against each are approximate and based on local market conditions and observations. The entrepreneur may find out the exact price from the concerned sources.						
The operative period of this Project is estimated to be about 10 years considering technology obsolesces.						
Implementation Schedule:						
i.	Purchase & Procurement of Machinery				2	WEEKS
ii.	Fabrication of Machinery & Transportation to Nigeria				12	WEEKS
iii.	Installation Commission & Production Trail				12	WEEKS
	Total:				26	WEEKS
Technical Aspects:						
Production Capacity:						
Rice Mill Plant XX ton/hour capacity (Input Paddy)						
Power required: YY KVA						

Financial Aspects of the Project: Fixed Capital						
Land - 2,50,000 Sqft						
Building:						
Machinery & Equipment:						
S. No.	Description			Length	Width	Height
1	Paddy Godown			250	75	25
2	Boiler Section			50	25	40
3	Dryer			Open-But Civil foundations are required		
4	Milling			150	100	45
5	Rice Godown			100	75	25
6	Store Room			100	50	25
7	Office+Panel Room+Other misc construction			10000 Square ft (Approx)		
The Total cost of Civil construction of land development, buildings and roads comes around =						A
Misc Cost for Transformer, APFC Panel, Cables, Lighting, Submersible, etc						B
Plant and Machinery =						C
Total Fixed Cost						D

Working Capital (per month):						
i) Personnel						
S. No.	Description	Nos	Salary	Total		
1	Manager	1				
2	Supervisor	4				
3	Skilled Worker	6				
4	Semi-skilled worker	6				
5	Helper	30				
6	Clerk	1				
7	Peon	1				
			Total	E		
Raw materials (per month):						
S. No.	Description		Qty (Ton)	Rate/ Ton	Value	
1	Paddy		F	G	FXG	
2	Poly Bags (In Pcs)		H	I	HXI	
3						
				Total	J	
Utilities (Per month):						

S. No.	Designation	Qty	Rate	Amount		
1	Electricity 800 KVA					
2	Water	2KLD/Day				
3	Husk	By Product of Milling		0		
4	Diesel	(Only required in case of electricity failure to run DG Set)				
			Total	K		
Other Contingent Expenses (per month):						
1	Postage and stationery					
2	Consumables					
3	Repair & maintenance					
4	Transport charges					
5	Advertisement & Publicity					
6	Insurance					
7	Miscellaneous expenditure					
	Total (Approx)			L		

Total Recurring Expenditure (Per/month):						
i.	Personnel		E			
ii.	Raw material		J			
iii.	Utilities		K			
iv.	Other Contingent Expenses		L			
	Total		M			
v.	Total Working Capital for 3 months:			3M		
Total Capital Investment:						
(i)	Fixed Capital		D			
(ii)	Working Capital		3M			
	Total		N			
Financial Analysis:						
Other Recurring Cost Per Annum						
S. No.	Particulars				Amount (USD)	
1	Depreciation on Machinery & Equipment @ 10%				O	

2	Interest on Capital Investment @ 12% pa.				P	
				Total	Q	
	Per Month:				Q/12=R	
Revenue Generation Per Month						
			Tons	Sold	Average Rate/Ton	Amount
Total production of Rice per month						
Total production of Husk						
Husk Available for sale						
Total production of Bran per month						
Impurity and non-recoverable losses						
					Total	S
Cost Per Month						
i.	Recurring Expenditure per Month		M			
ii.	Interest + Depreciation		R			
		Total	T			
Profit per Month			T-S	USD		
ROI = Total Capital Investment/Profit per month				Months		

Chapter 5

Foolproof Execution Plan

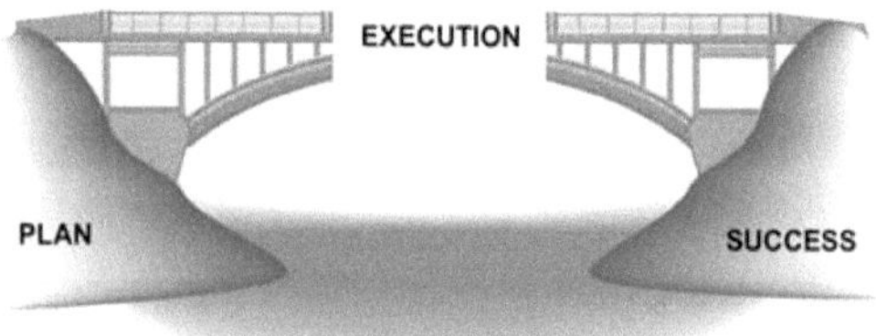

Rice Mill Project Execution Plan (RMPEP) is a governing document that defines how a project is to be executed, monitored, and controlled. It establishes exactly how the project execution phase will be managed to meet the requirements of the Project or contract.

Parts of a Rice Mill Project Execution Plan

The Project Execution Plan can include many activities and attributes. However, some essential project execution items should be included in every RMPEP.

1. **Project Goals and Objectives:** If you are driving a car and you don't know your destination, where will you go? Similarly, it is important to define your Project Goals to plan everything accordingly.

i. What will be the Milling capacity of the Project (Note-Capacity is always calculated in terms of Raw Paddy the plant will process per hour, i.e. Tons/hour or TPH)?

ii. What variety of Paddy will be processed?

iii. Government or Private supply? (because both have different requirements)

iv. Where and how the marketing will be done? (Add your own questions and research and write answers in detail, more questions you ask from yourself, more clarity you will start getting)

2. **Project Stakeholders:** Write the name of all stakeholders like partners, teammates, consultants, suppliers, contractors.
3. **Clearly Defined Responsibility & Scope of Work:** Define responsibilities to all stakeholders and define the scope of work in detail to avoid confusion, chaos, and dispute later.
4. **The Work Breakdown Structure (WBS) or how to manage Workflow for all Project Tasks:** Break down the entire Project into different activities, divide each activity into micro activities and manage the entire Project's workflow, as there are many interdependent activities.
5. **The Cost Breakdown Structure:** Prepare a cost breakdown of each micro activity and keep comparing it with the planned Budget.
6. **KPIs (Key Performance Indicators) that are to be tracked and reported:** Clearly define quantifiable measurement (key performance indicators) to gauge the performance of teammates and contractors and check it periodically.

7. **Risk Management Plan, including a list of possible risks and their Mitigation Plan:** Write down all the risks involved with the Project and prepare a Mitigation Plan.

   Example:

Risk	Mitigation Plan
The Budget may exceed than planned	Keep a Contingency Plan/ Budget
Chances of an accident at the site	Ask the contractors to cover their people in insurance. Buy insurance for your team as well.
Delayed supply of machinery	Cover it with a penalty clause
- - - - - - - - - - - - -	- - - - - - - - - - - - -

8. **Communications Plan, including what is to be communicated, to whom and when:** Lack of communication leads to confusion among team members & creates chaos. Technology has made information flow and communication very easy now. You can make different WhatsApp groups for it.
9. **Clearly defined Milestones and the process for verifying when Milestones are reached:** Follow the table management table provided in chapter 2.
10. **Clearly defined Gateway Review Process:** Make a weekly review system and take required action on tasks failing the expectations in terms of quality, cost and time (QCD).

The Rice Mill Project Execution Plan (RMPEP) is the basis for the success of a project. It defines how the Project will succeed and provides the path for getting there, driving better cost control, risk readiness, and project delivery.

Breakdown the entire Project into Activities (defined in the Time Management Table in chapter 2).

Prepare Execution Plan for each activity as per the following Table:

1. Activity - Company Registration

Micro Activity	Responsibility	Scope of work	Budget	Timeline	Documentation Required
Business Entity Registration (like Pvt Ltd, OPC, LLP, Proprietor, Public Ltd.)					
Udyog Aadhar					
Factory License					
NOC from Pollution Department					
GST					
PFA & ESIC					
FSSAI					
IEC (Import Export Code)					

Chapter 6

Layout Planning

Layout Planning decides on the best physical arrangement of all resources that consume space within a facility.

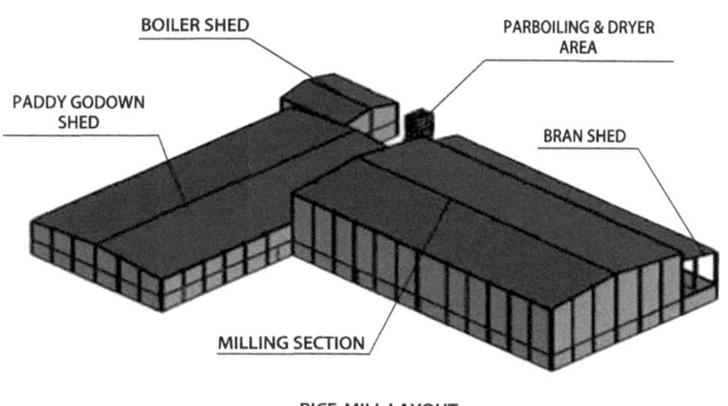

RICE-MILL LAYOUT

Layout Planning is crucial because it can significantly affect productivity and service quality. Some consequences of poor layout are increased costs, confused and frustrated teams, and poor communication and information flow.

The advantages of a good layout are:

- Improves Productivity.

- Improves quality. (Good layout ensures reduced movement of Paddy and Rice and thus reduced broken % age).
- Helps in better control and Synchronization of all processes (like Boiler, Parboiling, Drying, Milling, Sorting, Grading and Packing).
- Reduce workforce requirements and ease up supervision work.
- Reduce power consumption.
- Ease of maintenance.
- Effective use of the available area.
- Reduced requirement of material handling equipment.
- Reduced accidents.
- And overall improved profitability.

The steps for designing process layouts are:

1. **Gather information about space needs, space availability, and closeness requirements of departments.**

Use the following Table

S.No.	Department	Area Required	Height	Characteristics
01	Truck scale			Preferably should be near the gates
02	Office space			Office block should also be near the entry gate
03	Powerhouse (Transformer, Genset, LT Panel, Meter room)			Near Roadside
04	Truck Bay			It can be made outside the company premises or near the gate
05	Inside Roads			As per requirement (Min 20ft wide roads are recommended)
06	Paddy Godown/ Silos			Space should be sufficient to store at least 2 months of stock
07	Husk Yard			Better if Closer to Milling
08	Boiler			Preferably Near to Parboiling & Dryer to control heat losses
09	Precleaning section			It should be in between Paddy Godown and Parboiling
10	Parboiling & Dryer (Including conditioning silos)			Near the Milling, better it is.

11	Milling (including Electrical Panel, Color Sorter and Packing			Height should be kept sufficient to ensure the minimum requirement of conveyors
12	Rice Godown			Near Milling and exit gate
13	Bran Room			Preferably backside of Milling room
14	Misc (Lab, Spare part Store, Maintenance Room, Bardana store)			Separate space should be kept for all.
15	Workers & Staff Quarters			

2. **Developing a Block Plan or schematic of the Layout:** After step 1, sketch a block plan covering all the required departments as shown below:

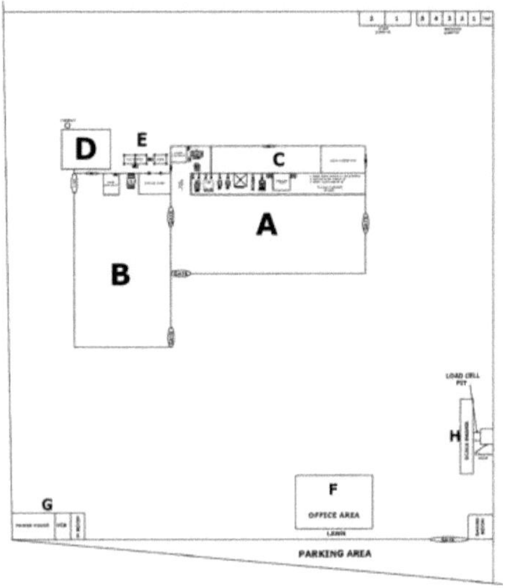

3. **Developing a detailed Layout:** After developing a block plan, make a detailed layout of each block as shown:

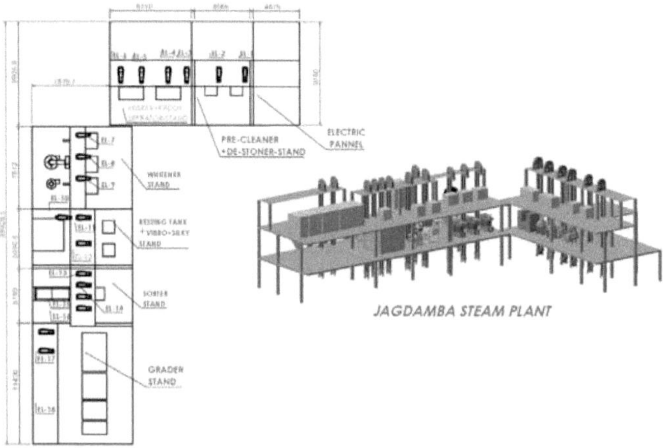

VASTU (the traditional Indian system of Architecture)

Vastu Shastra are texts on the traditional Indian system of architecture. These texts describe principles of design, layout, measurements, ground preparation, space arrangement, and spatial geometry. The designs aim to integrate architecture with nature, the relative functions of various parts of the structure, and ancient beliefs utilizing geometric patterns, symmetry, and directional alignments.

Vastu is the science of keeping five elements of nature in their proper positions.

10 Vastu Tips for Rice Mill

1. **Slope of Land in and around the industrial shed Slope should be towards the North or North-East.**

As per plot Vastu rules, an industrial plot-sloping downwards to the North or North-East is considered the best.

The earth's magnetic field flows from the North-East towards the South-West. A slope towards the North-East is thus beneficial to take the best advantage of the magnetic flow.

On the other hand, an industrial plot with a slope towards the South or South-West is certainly not advisable.

Similarly, while planning the Vastu for an industrial shed, do remember that the shed's roof should slope towards the North or East for the rainwater to flow.

2. **Heat Generating Devices & Electrical Devices:** Electrical Control Panels, Transformers, Generators & Boilers are standard assets in every Rice Mills. Their placement also plays a key role in the smooth functioning of the production process.

   As per Vastu Shastra, placement of the electrical equipment like transformers and control panels is an essential part of Factory Vastu. These electrical equipments represent the fire element.

   It is advisable to place boilers in the South and South-East (fire zones) as per Factory Vastu.

   If they are wrongly placed in zones like the North or North-East, they can seriously jeopardize production.

   A Generator is also a piece of electrical equipment, but its purpose is to provide electrical backup in case of an electrical breakdown. Thus, the ideal location of a generator should be in the North-West.

3. **Machines:** machines such as the heaviest/highest machinery should come in the South-West corner. In the Rice Mill Parboiling & Dryer process is the highest as well as the heaviest part.
4. **Main Gate & Compound Walls/Boundary:** The factory main gate in all four directions can be good provided it is in the correct position. The following image on Vastu for the factory main gate indicates the best locations for the factory entrance.

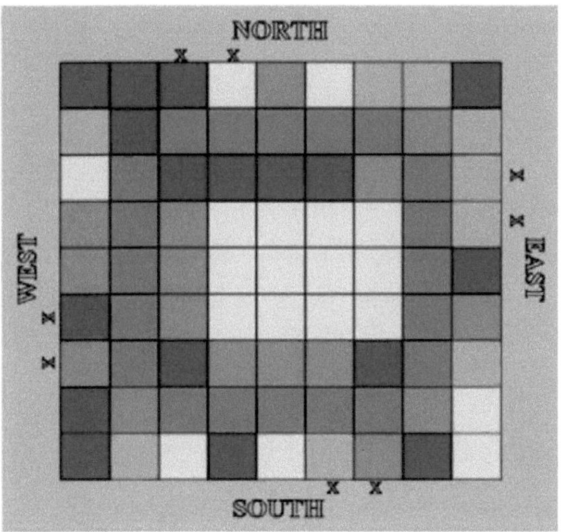

As per industrial Vastu, the auspiciousness of a factory depends not only on its facing direction but also on the location of its main gate and all other structures within the plot.

It is essential to keep in mind that the boundary walls in the South and West of the shed should be higher and thicker than those towards the North and the East.

This is because the path of the Sun is from East to West via South and South-West.

Around late afternoon and before sunset, the heat of the Sun is at its peak. When the Sun is in the South and South-West, there's an increase in the ultraviolet radiation in the atmosphere. This causes a natural disruption of the energy patterns.

On the contrary, lower and thinner walls in the North and East help absorb the beneficial infrared rays in the morning and early afternoon.

5. **Location of the Owner's Cabin:** As a general rule, the owners' office is ideal in the West or the South directions.

   West is the direction of overall gains and profits. On the other hand, the South can bring name, fame, and an authoritative position in the industry.

6. **Location of the Staff Cabins & Labor Quarters:** Since the success of a Rice Mill is heavily dependent on the staff & workers, one should carefully decide on their placement.

   It is best to construct the labor quarter towards the South-East corner of the shed. This is because the fiery energies of this direction will keep the labor motivated and energized to perform well.

   A technical machine operator's cabin should be in the South-West. Such a placement will ensure that the technical staff sharpens their skills over time.

   On the other hand, the shed's administrative area should ideally be located in the East direction. This being the direction of Sun will give him the necessary skills of control and administration.

The South of South-East is the ideal location for the placement of the guard room.

7. **Placement of the Raw Materials and Finished Goods:** The most important components of a Rice Mill are its raw materials (Paddy) and the finished goods (Rice). That is what the Rice Mill survives on. Thus, it is essential to choose their placement correctly.

   It is best to place all the raw materials (Paddy) in the West Zone of the Factory.

   North-West is the best direction for the placement of finished goods (Rice Bags).

   This direction ensures continuous movement and flow of the finished goods.

   The North-West, called the Vayavya Koan, has the energies of the Vayu Tattva or the air element. The quality of the air element is constant flow; this direction ensures that a regular flow and movement of the finished goods is maintained.

8. **Placement of Water Boring, Toilets and Septic Tank:** North, North-East and East are the best directions for the placement of a water boring facility in a factory. These are the directions that support the water element-the representative of growth and opportunities.

   On the contrary, overhead water tanks represent the earth element. Therefore, they should ideally be placed in the South-West or West zones while doing Vastu for factories. Do keep in mind that no overhead tanks should be placed in the North-East of the Factory.

A toilet or a septic tank in a factory is used to dispose of the waste solids and liquids.

Thus, the ideal locations for a septic tank and toilets in Vastu are the South of South-West or the West of North-West.

9. **Parking Area for Vehicles:** As per industrial Vastu rules, there should be separate parking spaces for heavy and light vehicles.

   The heavy vehicles parking must be outside the factory premises.

   If it's necessary to park them inside, it must be done in the South and South-West zones.

   Parking for lighter vehicles like cars, scooters or bicycles is best in the North-West direction. It can even be in the North and East zones of the Factory.

   It is advisable to avoid any parking in the North-East.

10. **Kitchen and Pantry Placement:** A mini representation of the cosmic fire, the kitchen or pantry in a factory must be placed correctly to balance the fire element. South-East to South are the ideal directions for the placement of a kitchen as per Vastu.

    One must avoid any black or blue wall paints, granite slabs or tiles in the kitchen. These colors represent the water element which is anti to the fire element of the kitchen.

Chapter 7

Team Selection

Even if you buy the best car but have a poor driver, it will result in a pathetic experience. The same is the case with Rice Mills.

Most of the time, the team selection process is missing in Rice mills, leading to loss of Productivity, Quality, and Frequent Machine Breakdowns.

The Selection Process involves the following steps:

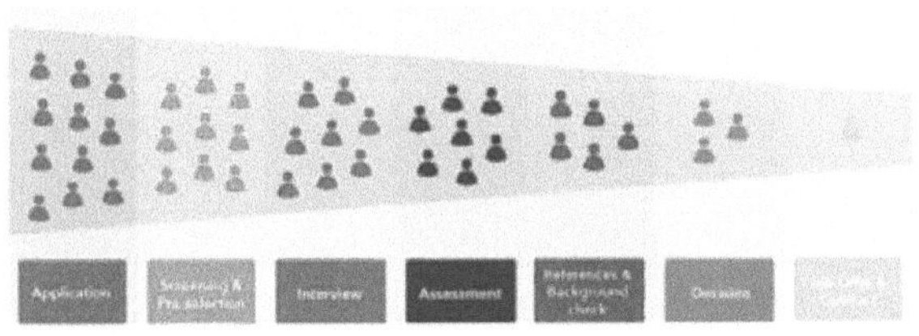

1. **Floating the needs (Application):** The first step in team selection is analyzing the needs.

Generally, the following team players are required in a Rice Mill:

i. Mill Operator/Supervisor
ii. Assistant Operator
iii. Maintenance In-Charge
iv. Boiler Operator.
v. Parboiling Operator.
vi. Color Sorter Operator.
vii. Store In-Charge.
viii. Lab In-Charge
ix. Accountant.
x. Manager
xi. Helpers

2. **Screening the Options:** Screen the available options and weed out the potential mismatch.
3. **Interview:** Prepare a list of questions for the candidates that best reveal the attitude and technical skills required for the job.

   The following questions can be put to the candidate being interviewed for the Mill Operator's job:

   i. How much is your experience?
   ii. How will you check the % age of broken Rice generated from any machine?
   iii. How will you measure the Productivity of any machine?

iv. What % age of Paddy should a Sheller machine Dehusk?

v. How can the whiteness of Rice coming from the Whitener Machine be increased or decreased?

vi. What Ampere of current is permissible for any motor in general?

vii. How will you check if the Elevator is returning the material?

viii. What can be the reason for the Destoner not removing the stones properly?

ix. What is the procedure for setting correction of Paddy Separator?

x. What will you check if broken Rice comes along with head Rice?

4. **Assessment:** After the interview, assess the capability of the candidates and select the most suitable person for the job.
5. **Reference and Background Check:** Ask the candidate to give you references and follow up on these. If you have doubts about a particular competency or skill during the interview, a reference check is an excellent way to gather more information.
6. **Decision:** The next step is deciding and choosing the candidate with the greatest future potential for the organization. Sometimes this means picking someone less qualified at the moment – but who is committed to growing and staying with the organization longer.

7. **Job Offer and Contract:** Once you have decided, make an offer to the candidate. If the offer is accepted, a contract is drawn up and signed. The selection process is completed only when all parties sign the employment contract.

Standard Appointment Letter format, change it as per your requirements:

Appointment Letter

29th Nov, 2021

Name: Mr. ....

Address: ....

Dear Mr. ....

This has reference to your application for employment in our organization and the subsequent interview with us. We are pleased to inform you that you have been selected as a team member. The details of which are as follows:

Designation:	Mill Supervisor
Joining Date:	01st Dec, 2022
Duty Timing:	9:00am 06:00pm
Work Area:	xxxxxx
Head office:	xxxxxx

Salary

A detailed brief on KRAs and scope of work will be given to you on joining. You will be entitled to a Gross Salary of Rs. xxxxxxxxx per month.

Place of Work

Your immediate posting will be at our Rice Mil\at xxxxxxxxx, and you will be governed by the rules and regulations of the company in force.

Annual Leave

You will be allowed leave as per the company's policy and regulations.

Probation

You will be on probation for a period of six months, and after successful completion of the probation period, your services can be confirmed by the Management in writing. In case you do not receive any letter in writing on completion of your probation period, you will be deemed to be on probation, but on completion of 12 months, your services are deemed to be confirmed in the organization.

Termination Notice

After confirmation, either Party may terminate this employment relationship by giving 1 months notice or by making payment of 1 month's compensation in lieu of notice or for the period falling short of the notice period.

Your employment may also be terminated without notice in the event of any serious grave misconduct.

The terms serious misconduct shall include conduct which in the reasonable opinion of the company is materially damaging to the business of the company or any conduct of the individual likely to bring the company into disrepute or any persistent non-observance of any terms and conditions of employment or continuous failure substantially to perform your duties or carry out your obligations.

Sole & Exclusive Occupation

You will devote your whole time and attention to the organization's business. You will not be interested or engaged directly or indirectly as an agent or employee for any other person, firm etc.

Property & Information

All instruction, documents, reports, data, and other information relating to the company's business that may come into your possession shall be the company's exclusive property, and you will not disclose the same to anyone.

Responsibility for Company's Work

You will take good care of the company's money, property or equipment that may be entrusted to you and shall be responsible for any damage or shortage, or loss of such money, property and equipment.

Discipline

During the tenure of your employment with the organization, you shall be governed by the rules and regulations applicable to your cadre. And all the time, you will maintain good discipline in the organization. The organization shall have the right to take disciplinary action if you are found indulging in riotous behavior affecting Workflow or threatening superiors or indulging in defamation of the company or of your superior, or committing any act which is likely to be detrimental to the interest of the company subversive of the discipline.

Personal

Any change in your current residential address must be immediately communicated to the company. All official communication would be made to the address last given by you in writing.

Medical Fitness

Your appointment is subject to your being medically fit in all respects during the employment.

Confidentiality

You agree at all times not to use for your advantage or disclose to any third party any information concerning the business or affairs of the company, comprising trade secrets and business matters or information which you know or ought to have known to be confidential.

Please confirm your acceptance of the above terms and conditions by signing and returning the duplicate copy of this employment letter.

Thanking you,

Yours Sincerely,

For XXXXX

(Authorized Signatory)

Bonus Chapter

Efficient Management of Rice Mill to Mint Money

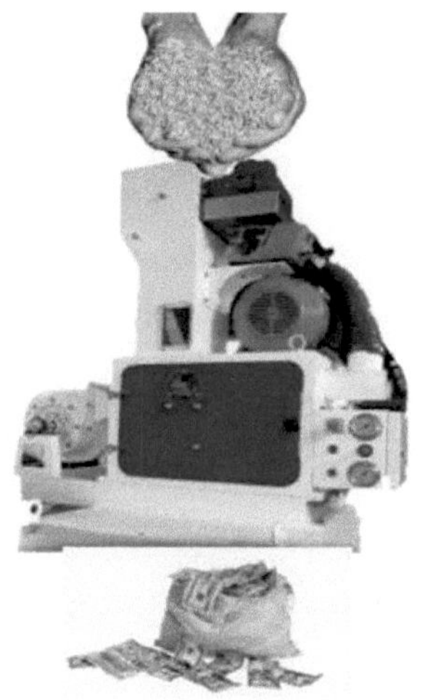

Despite the best selection of machines and workforce, many Rice Mills suffer losses and shut down each year.

Apart from external factors (like poor demand, government policies and price fluctuations), the core reason is poor management by the Promoter.

If the Rice Mill is managed efficiently, it can mint money and contribute to society by generating employment and catering to the food requirement.

Though I will cover this in detail in my next book, I am sharing bullet points here that the promoters need to take care of.

1. **Paddy Procurement:** Maintain standard operating procedures and all related documents.
2. **Lab inspection of Paddy:** Maintain standard operating procedures and all related documents.
3. **Storage:** Maintain standard operating procedures and all related documents.
4. **Cleaning, Parboiling, Drying:** Maintain standard operating procedures and all related documents.
5. **Milling:** Maintain standard operating procedures and all related documents.
6. **Things to be monitored - Making a Dashboard:** If you don't have a dashboard in your car, you will not know the speed at which you are driving and either you will go too slow to reach your destination on time, or you will be driving very fast and have an accident. Similarly, a dashboard is required for the Rice Mill.
7. **Maintenance:** Routine maintenance reduces the breakdown and enhances the life of machines.
8. **Accounting, Cash Flow Management and Profit Monitoring:** Cash Flow is the lifeblood for a Rice Mill, and profit is the reward for taking so much effort and risk to run it.

9. **Team Management:** Teams should be aligned with the organization goals and objectives, and promoters should ensure their growth and development.
10. **Rice Storage, Packing, Branding & Marketing:** Proper Packing, Branding and Marketing work like a magnet, and it attracts possible customers to buy your Rice.

Call To Action

Dear friends, I hope I was able to add to your knowledge about Rice Mill Project Planning. I decided to create this book after noticing a gap between the reality and the knowledge that most aspiring rice millers have.

By sharing our knowledge with others in the industry, we were able to save billions of valuable assets of our nation and speed up the return on investment. I have written this book to serve the nation and humanity and to contribute in some way to my bigger goal of serving towards a starvation free world.

Our company is a socially responsible organization, and we are contributing towards literacy by establishing libraries in many small schools. We have contributed to an Operation Theatre in the Shri Satya Sai Charitable hospital in Palwal. We are also part of the Life-Savers group, where we try to help the needy with blood emergencies.

I hope I have been able to add value to your knowledge. If you want to know more about Rice Mill Projects, you are most welcome to connect with me.

Our team of experts can visit your site and guide you on how to establish your Rice Mill Project without any errors.

Further, we are available on:

Web: www.agromachengineering.com.

Mobile no.- +91 8800899179, +91 9910109153

WHY AGROMACH

1. We have fully integrated manufacturing facilities.
2. Our facility includes imported technology from Japan (Laser Cutting, CNC Bending Machine).
3. We have all types of welding machines (Mig, Tig, Arc, Spot)
4. State of the art powder coating plant and Shot blasting unit for good surface finish and better life of end product.
5. CNC turning machine for manufacturing all types of shaft and other machining items with minimum error.
6. We have our design and development centre with the latest licensed softwares like Solid work and Solid cam with a trained team of engineers to work on them.
7. We have a dedicated team of engineers in the manufacturing and quality control departments.
8. We have the latest ERP software to track the proper flow of work from order booking to dispatch.
9. We provide complete hand holding in select human reprocessing, human resources, layout designing, and other project planning attributes.
10. We have a strong value system. We believe in doing what is right for the customer "If our product is of no value to you, then your money is of no value to us."
11. We are proud to be the only company in our segment that offers a 100%money-back guarantee (within 60 days).
12. Highly dedicated team and prompt after-sale support.
13. We are ISO 9001:2015 and ISO 14001:2015 Certified Company.
14. We have 500+ satisfied customers and are trusted by world leaders.
15. We have an experienced and trained team for handling turnkey projects.

Printed by Libri Plureos GmbH in Hamburg,
Germany